PATTERNS AND PUZZLES

LEARNING RESOURCES®

Sharpen your students' problem-solving skills with activities from these other helpful publications. For a Learning Resources® dealer near you, call (800) 222-3909.

Problem Solving with Pentominoes

Introduce and teach the mathematics of this challenging 12-piece puzzle. Easy-to-follow 96-page activity book features blackline masters, teaching notes, and handy class management features. Topics include pentomino shapes, motions, tessellations, symmetry, congruence, similarity, perimeter, area, and puzzle challenges. Grades 1–4.

LER 414

ISBN 1-56911-999-6

Shapes Alive! by Neville Leeson

Keep your students' problem-solving skills in tip-top shape! 96-page blackline master book is loaded with geometric puzzles and problem-solving activities using tangrams, pentominoes, geoboards, geometric solids, and protractors. Grades 3–6.

LER 467

ISBN 1-56911-000-X

Tangrams in Action Binder

This resource binder puts everything at your fingertips — Tangrams included! 128-page binder takes a cooperative learning approach with detailed teaching notes and blackline masters *plus one Overhead and four student Tangrams!* Topics include geometry, spatial sense, problem solving, area, perimeter, similarity, and congruence. Perfect for your Math Activity Center. Grades K-4.

LER 519

ISBN 1-56911-993-7

PATTERNS
AND PUZZLES

Mathematical challenges
for grades 3 and 4

Neville Leeson

Published with the permission of Dellasta Pty. Ltd.

© revised 1993 Learning Resources, Inc., Lincolnshire, Illinois 60069.

First published 1990 by Dellasta Pty. Ltd., Mount Waverley, Victoria, Australia.

ISBN 1-56911-001-8 (previously ISBN 0-947138-44-7)

Printed in the United States of America.

CONTENTS

EXPLORING NUMBER PATTERNS

For each example, complete the number sentences, look for a pattern and then write the next two lines of the pattern:

a
$1 + 2 =$
$2 + 3 =$
$3 + 4 =$
$4 + 5 =$

b
$2 \times 3 =$
$3 \times 4 =$
$4 \times 5 =$
$5 \times 6 =$

c
$1 + 3 =$
$3 + 5 =$
$5 + 7 =$

d
$2 + 4 =$
$4 + 6 =$
$6 + 8 =$

e
$1 \times 3 - 1 =$
$2 \times 3 - 1 =$
$3 \times 3 - 1 =$

f
$1^2 + 1 =$
$2^2 + 2 =$
$3^2 + 3 =$

Exploring number patterns — continued

g　2^2 − 1 =　　　　**h**　1 × 3 =

　　3^2 − 1 =　　　　　　3 × 5 =

　　4^2 − 1 =　　　　　　5 × 7 =

i　0^2 + 0 + 1 =

　　1^2 + 1 + 2 =

　　2^2 + 2 + 3 =

HIT THE TARGET

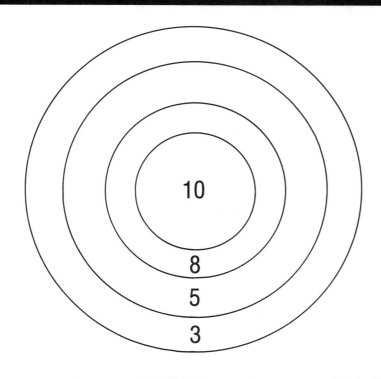

1 Sue took three shots at this target and scored 19. Where did her shots land?

2 If Bob scored 20 from three shots, where could his shots have landed?

3 If Mary scored 22 from five shots, where could her shots have landed?

FIND THEM

2	8	3	4	2	1
4	5	3	9	1	3
3	1	0	6	5	3
5	3	3	2	4	2
1	6	0	7	1	3
8	7	4	2	6	0

Find and circle all the pairs of numbers with a sum of 6:

DEEP SEA DIVE

Fill in the missing spaces to find the secret number to unlock the treasure chest.

ADDITION SEARCH

3	5	8	7	2	3
1	7 + 5 = 12			9	6
4	6	10	4	11	15
7	8	8	16	5	21
3	14	9	7	16	5
10	7	17	4	21	8

Find as many addition number sentences as possible. (Numbers may be used more than once.)

MULTIPLICATION SEARCH

2	8	16	3	6	20
7	4	5	8	9	4
4	32	1	24	54	27
28	8	25	30	7	9
14	7	6	42	3	15
10	5	8	48	21	90

Find as many multiplication number sentences as possible. (Numbers can be used more than once. Number sentences can be formed horizontally, vertically, or diagonally.)

THREE IN A LINE

Play this game with a friend:

1   Obtain or make two dice, each with 4, 5, 6, 7, 8, 9 on their faces.

2   Copy or use the playing board below.

3   Each player should obtain a supply of markers (e.g. red for one player and blue for the other).

4   Flip a coin to decide who goes first.

5   In turn the players roll the two dice and cover a number on the board that is the sum of the two top numbers on the dice.

6   The winner is the player who first covers three numbers in a line.

(As a variation, the winner could be the first player to cover four numbers either in a line or in a square shape.)

18	10	13	14	9
11	17	11	16	15
15	9	12	10	12
13	14	12	13	8
12	16	11	17	14

THREE OF A KIND

Make each sentence true by putting in the correct signs. The first one has been done for you.

THREE TWOS

$(2 - 2) \times 2 = 0$

$2 \quad 2 \quad 2 = 6$

$2 \quad 2 \quad 2 = 8$

$2 \quad 2 \quad 2 = 2$

THREE THREES

$3 \quad 3 \quad 3 = 9$

$3 \quad 3 \quad 3 = 3$

$3 \quad 3 \quad 3 = 2$

$3 \quad 3 \quad 3 = 6$

$3 \quad 3 \quad 3 = 12$

$3 \quad 3 \quad 3 = 18$

$3 \quad 3 \quad 3 = 0$

$3 \quad 3 \quad 3 = 27$

$3 \quad 3 \quad 3 = 4$

THREE FOURS

$4 \quad 4 \quad 4 = 12$

$4 \quad 4 \quad 4 = 4$

$4 \quad 4 \quad 4 = 20$

$4 \quad 4 \quad 4 = 64$

$4 \quad 4 \quad 4 = 32$

$4 \quad 4 \quad 4 = 2$

$4 \quad 4 \quad 4 = 0$

THREE FIVES

$5 \quad 5 \quad 5 = 15$

$5 \quad 5 \quad 5 = 5$

$5 \quad 5 \quad 5 = 20$

$5 \quad 5 \quad 5 = 30$

$5 \quad 5 \quad 5 = 2$

$5 \quad 5 \quad 5 = 50$

$5 \quad 5 \quad 5 = 125$

$5 \quad 5 \quad 5 = 0$

PATTERNS AND SEQUENCES

1 Use square tiles to make this pattern:

☐ , ☐☐ , ☐☐☐

Make the next three.
Write it down as a number sequence

___ , ___ , ___ , ___ , ___ , ___

What is the rule?

2 Form this pattern:

☐ , ☐☐ , ☐☐/☐☐ , ☐☐☐☐/☐☐☐☐

Write it down as a number sequence

___ , ___ , ___ , ___ , ___ , ___

What is the rule?

3 Form this:

☐ , ☐☐/☐☐ , ☐☐☐/☐☐☐/☐☐☐

Write the number sequence

___ , ___ , ___ , ___ , ___ , ___

What is the rule?

4 Form this:

☐ , ☐/☐☐ , ☐/☐☐/☐☐☐

Write the number sequence

___ , ___ , ___ , ___ , ___ , ___

What is the rule?

BUILDING BRIDGES

Play this game with a friend:

1 Flip a coin to decide who goes first.

2 Each player uses a different colored pencil and, in turn, connects two numbers from adjacent columns (i.e. from columns next to each other).

3 A player scores one point every time he or she connects three numbers (one from each column) whose sum is 25. A number can only be used once to form a sum of 25; it cannot be used again with a different pair of numbers. Lines connecting winning numbers may cross other lines. (A player can try to prevent the other from obtaining a sum of 25 by using the number needed.)

4 The winner is the first player to score 3 points or the one with the most points when all numbers have been used.

22	3	6
6	8	7
11	12	10
19	15	19
8	20	9
23	1	15
17	9	20
4	19	18
7	4	16
9	2	8
12	6	1
16	11	2
13	14	5
5	16	23
10	21	13
15	10	4
14	5	17
3	18	3
2	23	11
18	7	14
20	13	21
1	17	12
21	22	22

NUMBER PUZZLES (1)

1 Find the secret message:

7 × 8	6 × 7	6 × 3	8 × 8
9 × 8	5 × 2	7 × 3	6 × 7
6 × 2	8 × 3	3 × 6	2 × 9
6 × 8	8 × 4	12 × 3	9 × 4

C	=	12	—	=	48	R	=	21	L	=	18

C = 12   — = 48   R = 21   L = 18
9 = 32   P = 64   A = 24   E = 42
H = 56   F = 72   I = 10   1 = 36

2 Which numbers do not belong:

31   43   309   81   34   35

18   903   13   63   120   77

3 Search for a pattern and then fill in the boxes:

4 Fill in the boxes in this addition sum:

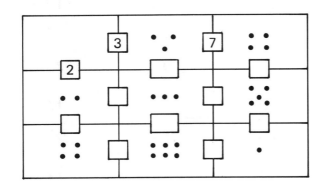

```
  5  0  2
  1  □  4
  2  6  □
  _____
  □  5  7
  _____
```

NUMBER PUZZLES (2)

1 Place each of the numbers 1 to 5 in the circles so that the sum of three numbers along each line is 9.

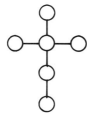

2 Place each of the numbers 1 to 6 in the circles so that all the lines add up to the same total. (Can you find more than one solution?)

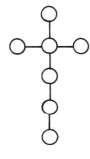

3 Now try the same using the numbers 1 to 7.

4 Place each of the numbers 1 to 6 in the circles so that each line has the same sum.

5 Place each of the numbers 1, 2, 3, 4, 6, 12 in these circles so that each line has the same product.

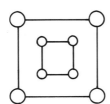

6 Place each of the numbers 1 to 8 in these circles so that the sum of the numbers for each square is the same.

NUMBER PUZZLES (3)

1 Move one tag to another box so that the sum for each is 15:

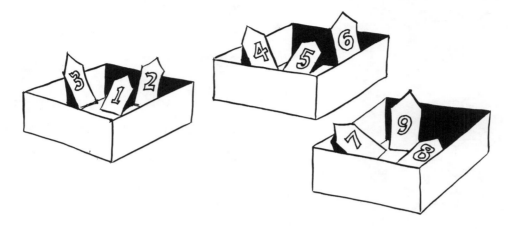

2 Study the pattern of the beads. How many beads are inside the box?

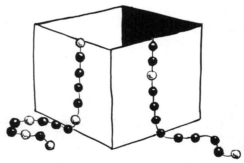

3 Place each of the numbers 1 to 6 in the boxes so that each circle has the same total:

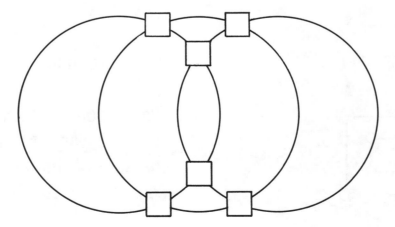

CUTTING A PIZZA

Complete this table:

	Number of cuts	Number of pieces
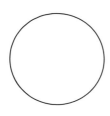	0	1
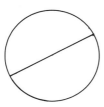	1	
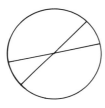	2	
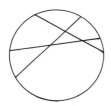	3	
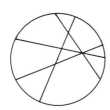	4	

Can you see a pattern?
How many pieces are there:
a for 5 cuts
b for 8 cuts?

EXPLORING WITH TANGRAMS

1 Trace or photocopy the diagram on this page and then cut out the seven pieces.

2 Jumble up the pieces and then try to reform the square without looking at this diagram.

3 Use the two small triangles (A and B) and the square (C) to form a triangle.

4 Can you make a triangle using the pieces A, B, and D? Now try using A, B, and E.

5 Can you make a triangle using A, B, C, and D?

6 What other shapes can you make using A, B, and C?

7 What shapes can you make using all seven pieces?

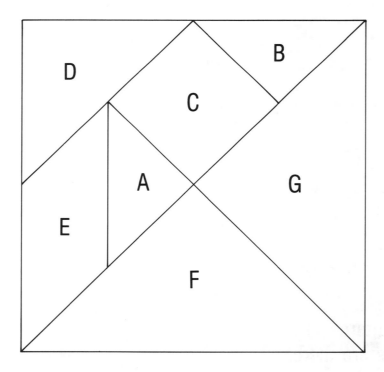

TANGRAM PUZZLES

Use your set of tangrams (from the previous activity) to cover each of these:

MATH PATH ADDITION

Study these two examples:

1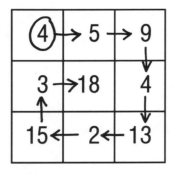

2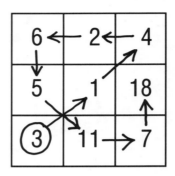

4 and 5 equals 9;   3 + 1 = 4;
9 and 4 equals 13;   4 + 2 = 6;
13 + 2 = 15;   6 + 5 = 11;
15 + 3 = 18.   11 + 7 = 18.

Now try these by putting in arrows:

a

8	1	7
3	11	4
20	5	15

b

11	2	18
4	3	9
15	8	1

c

5	9	5
5	14	4
19	5	24

d

4	4	17
6	13	3
10	3	20

Can you complete **e**
this one:

4		7
	15	
19		12

TARGET PRIME

This is a game for two, three, or four players.

1 Obtain three dice numbered 1 to 6.

2 By flipping a coin (or rolling a die) decide who goes first.

3 Each player, in turn, rolls the three dice and, using the three numbers on the top faces, tries to obtain a prime number, by adding, subtracting and/or multiplying the numbers on the dice, e.g. using numbers 2, 3, 5 you can obtain $3 \times 5 + 2 = 17$.

4 The winner is the first player to obtain five different prime numbers.

STRIKE OFF

Play this game with a friend:

1 Each player should write the numbers 1 to 12 on a piece of paper.

2 Obtain two dice numbered 1 to 6.

3 Flip a coin to decide who plays first.

4 Each player, in turn, rolls the two dice and then crosses off any two numbers that add to the sum on the dice or crosses off one number equal to the sum, e.g. if you roll a sum of 7, you may cross off 1 and 6, or 2 and 5, or 3 and 4, or just 7. (You may use one die when the sum of the numbers remaining is less than 6.)

5 The winner is the first player to cross off all twelve numbers. (Each player has only one turn at a time, regardless of whether numbers may be crossed off or not.)

SAND TRAP

Play this game with a friend:

1   Use a die marked 1, 1, 2, 2, 3, 3 and a board like the one shown. Each player will need one token.

2   Flip a coin to decide who goes first.

3   Players, in turn, roll the die twice. The first throw shows moves across to the right and the second shows moves up. A player who lands in a trap (☐) must return to Start.

4   The winner is the first player to reach the top or side of the Forest (either by throwing the exact number or a higher number than is needed).

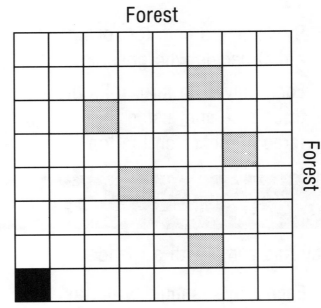

Forest

Start

RACE TO ONE

Play this game with a friend:

1   Flip a coin to decide who goes first.

2   First player chooses any number between 20 and 100, e.g. 56.

3   Second player subtracts from it one of its factors, e.g. 56 − 8 = 48.

4   First player subtracts a factor of the new number, e.g. 48 − 4 = 44.

5   Players, in turn, continue to subtract factors, e.g. 44 − 11 = 33, etc.

6   The player who obtains 1 wins.

POLY-COLOR

Play this game with a friend:

1 Copy (or invent) a map of a country with states (or regions).

2 Use a die with 1, 1, 2, 2, 3, 3 on its faces. Roll the die to find how many colors (one, two, or three) may be used in the game.

3 Flip a coin to decide who goes first.

4 Players, in turn, choose any of the colors and shade any state on the map. Players cannot use the same color to shade adjacent states (states that have a common border).

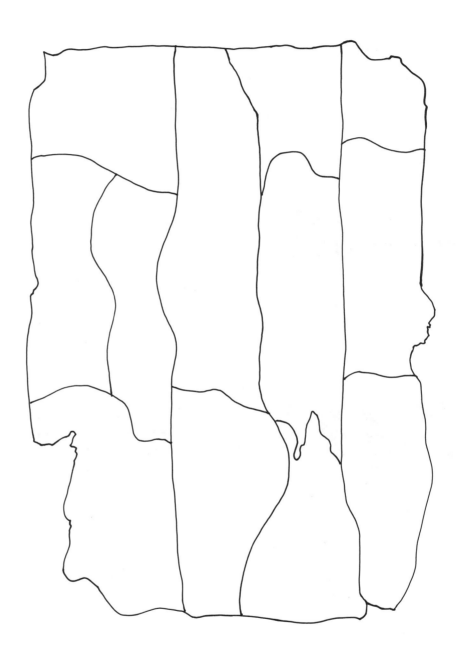

5 The winner is the last player able to shade a state.

Note: For your first game you might like to use this map:

FIND THE WINNER

Pam, Sue, Bob, Jill and Rick are running in a sack race. Part-way through the race they are in these positions:

Pam is 30 meters behind Sue.
Sue is 50 meters ahead of Rick.
Bob is 30 meters ahead of Rick.
Jill is 30 meters ahead of Bob.

Who at this stage is winning? Who is coming in second?

HOW MANY STEPS?

A fireman stood on the middle step of a ladder. As the smoke cleared, he climbed up 3 steps. The fire got worse so he had to climb down 6 steps. Then he climbed up the last 8 steps and was at the top of the ladder. How many steps were in the ladder?

WHAT CAN SHE BUY?

Betty has a $20 bill. Which of these purchases can she make?

a   3 meters of material at $5.98 per meter.

b   A pattern for $5.65 plus 4 meters of material at $4.25 per meter.

c   5 balls of wool at $2.80 per ball and 2 sets of buttons at $2.15 per set.

d   3 meters of lace at $3.95 per meter plus 2 meters of material at $4.55 per meter.

WHAT AM I?

1 I am a number between 30 and 40.
My units digit is double my tens digit.
What am I?

2 I am a number between 20 and 30.
I have six factors (other than myself and 1).
What am I?

3 I am the shape of a traffic stop sign.
What am I?

4 I am a number between 20 and 30.
I am a square number.
What am I?

BREAK THE CODE

1 If is 146

and is 305

what is ?

2 If equals 2031

and equals 3211

what does equal?

DOT PAPER SHAPES

On the dot paper below draw these:

a   A five-sided figure

b   A square with an area of 4 square units

c   A rectangle with an area of 6 square units

d   A different shape (not a rectangle) with an area of 6 square units

e   A four-sided figure with exactly one axis of symmetry

f   A six-sided shape with exactly 2 axes of symmetry.

A six-sided shape with an area of 3 square units is shown as an example.

FURTHER NUMBER PUZZLES (1)

1 Start at A and draw a path to B so that the sum of the numbers is 20. You can only travel down and across (either to the right or to the left).

		A↓		
2	1	1	2	1
1	3	2	4	1
2	3	4	1	3
1	2	1	3	2
4	1	2	4	3
		↓B		

2 Can you complete the square so that there is a 1, 2, 3, 4 and 5 in each column and in each row?

1	4	3	2	5
4				
3				
2				
5				

3 Put a number in each space so that each number sentence is correct:

5	+		−		=6
×		×		−	
	+		−		=2
+		−		+	
	×		−		=0
=9		=10		=9	

FURTHER NUMBER PUZZLES (2)

1 Place each of the numbers
1 to 4 in the squares so that:
- the top row contains odd
  numbers only;
- the second column
  contains square numbers only.

2 Place each of the numbers
1 to 6 so that:
- the first column has even
  numbers;
- the sum of the second
  column is 3;
- the sum of the first row is 8.

3 Place each of the numbers
1 to 6 so that:
- the sum of the top row is 9;
- the sum of the bottom row is 12;
- the sum of each column is 7.

4 Place each of the numbers
1, 2, 3, 4, 5, 6, 7, 8, 9 in the
empty spaces to give the
sums shown.

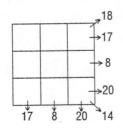

5 Place each of the numbers
1 to 8 in the squares so that
no two consecutive numbers
(numbers that follow each
other) are in squares next to
each other or in squares that
meet in a point.

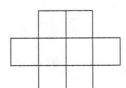

FURTHER NUMBER PUZZLES (3)

1 I am an odd number.
I am between 20 and 30.
The sum of my digits is 5.
What number am I?

2 How much is:
$9 \times 8 \times 7 \times 6 \times 5 \times 4 \times 3 \times 2 \times 1 \times 0$?

3 What is an archaeologist? An archaeologist claimed that he found a coin dated 87 B.C. Do you think he did?

4 What number am I? I am a two-digit, odd, composite number less than 20.

5 There are two identical jars: one is full of nickels, the other is half-full of dimes. Which would you prefer?

6 A bag contains 20 buttons colored red, white, and blue.

There are 6 more red than white, and 3 times as many white as blue. How many of each are there?

7 Can you calculate this shopping bill, given the clue that K = 6?

J pencils at J cents each	KL ¢
K pens at J cents each	LJ ¢
Q books at KL cents each	$P.QJ
Total	$Q.LO

8 A man found a wallet containing four bills. The total amount of money was $25. What were the four bills?

FIND THE PATTERN

In each find the missing number:

a			**b**			**c**		
2	6		2	14		7	13	
5	9		9	63		3	5	
7	11		4	28		5	9	
4	8		7	49		4	7	
8	12		3	?		2	3	
3	?					8	?	

d			**e**		
3	10		5	24	
8	25		2	3	
5	16		6	35	
6	19		3	8	
1	4		4	?	
4	?				

NUMBERS FOR LETTERS

Replace the letters with numbers in these addition examples:

a		**b**		**c**		**d**		**e**	
A B		A B		4 A B		A B C		A B C	
1 4		C D		B C 2		A B C		A B C	
7 A		5 7		C 8 A		E D A		D C E F	

FIND THE WORD

Complete each of the additions and put the letter in the box where the answer would occur on the number line:

E: 48 + 24 = 72   R: 18 + 9 =   C: 68 + 35 =

I: 47 + 47 =   I: 19 + 14 =   A: 7 + 8 =

T: 28 + 16 =   T: 77 + 9 =   M: 44 + 19 =

H: 27 + 27 =

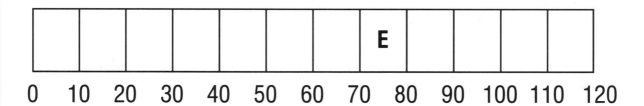

							E					

0   10   20   30   40   50   60   70   80   90   100   110   120

CHOOSING COINS

Circle the coins that will add up to the total at the bottom of each column:

1	1	1	1	1	1
1	1	1	1	1	1
5	5	5	5	5	5
5	5	5	5	5	5
10	10	10	10	10	10
25	25	25	25	25	25
25	25	25	25	25	25
—	—	—	—	—	—
31¢	51¢	40¢	21¢	46¢	66¢
—	—	—	—	—	—

HIDDEN NUMBERS

What digit is under each pancake?

The sum of column 2 is 7

Column 1 total equals row 3 total

Numbers in row 1 are factors of 30

The sum of row 1 is 9

The sum of column 3 is 20

Each of the numbers 1–9 appears under the pancakes

Four corners are odd numbers

Numbers in column 1 are factors of 18

FIND WHAT IS WRONG

1

STOP

2

SUPER SALE!

Suits $\frac{1}{2}$ Price

~~$300~~

$200

3

3:40

4

Cube

Cone

Triangular Prism

FOLD AND CUT

1 Fold a square piece of paper in half, then in half again.
Cut off the corner (where the double fold is).
Can you guess what figure is formed?
Open out the paper and check.
Try this a few times. Do you always obtain the same kind of figure?

2 Fold a piece of paper in half, then in half again.
What angle is the corner (where the double fold is)?
Halve this angle by folding one edge of it onto the other.
Now cut off the corner (where the triple fold is).
Can you guess what shape is formed?
Open out the paper to check.

DRAWING CIRCLES

1 In how many ways can you draw a circle?

2 Try these:
a Obtain a circle by tracing around a cylinder.
b Draw a circle using a compass.
c Draw a circle using a pencil, a piece of string and a thumb tack.

d Can you obtain a circle using your span (distance from tip of thumb to tip of little finger of outstretched hand)?
e Can you think of other ways of forming circles?

3 Find out what concentric circles are. Draw some.

4 Make a pattern with circles (or parts of circles).

SHAPES FROM SQUARES

1 Copy these two squares onto a piece of paper and cut out each one:

2 Can you make a symmetrical shape by placing these two squares so that they have at least one point in common (i.e. so that they touch at a point or in a line)?

3 How many different symmetrical shapes can you make in this manner?

WHERE ARE THEY?

Three models (a tower, a tree, and a car) were placed in the squares of this board:

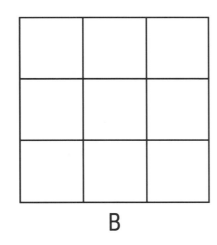

The view from side A of the board is:

The view from side B is:

Where were the models placed?

NUMBER COVER

This is a game for two to four players.

1 Each player has a board like the one below. [You could copy it onto a piece of paper.]

2 Use three dice with faces labeled 1 to 6.

3 Roll a die to decide who goes first.

4 Players, in turn, roll the three dice and use the three numbers on them to form a number sentence for any number on their board, e.g. $(3 + 4) \times 2 = 14$ or $2 \times 4 + 3 = 11$. This number is then covered.

5 The winner is the first player to cover all the numbers on his or her board.

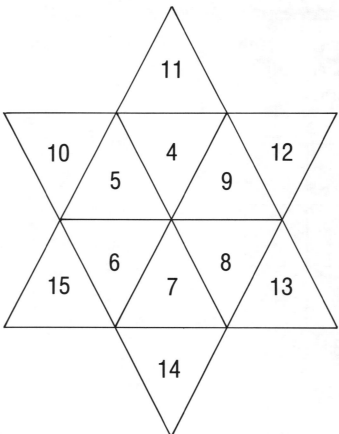

LUNCH ORDERS

Pam, Sue, and Nick ordered their lunches from this menu:

MENU			
Pizza slice	$2.00	Drink	72¢
Salad	$1.95	Juice	45¢
Egg roll	85¢	Cake	75¢
Taco	$1.05	Apple	65¢
Vegetarian pie	90¢	Pear	55¢

Complete their lunch orders:

Pam

Pizza slice $2.00

_____ _____

_____ _____

$3.00

Sue

_____ _____

_____ _____

_____ _____

$3.42

Nick

_____ _____

_____ _____

_____ _____

$1.90

A MAGIC SQUARE

1 What is the sum of each row?

2 What is the sum of each column?

3 What is the sum of each diagonal?

4 Notice that the sum of 8 and 2 is 10; so is the sum of 1 and 9. Can you find any more?

5 The sum of 1 and 3 is double 2; the sum of 1 and 7 is double 4. Can you see more like this?

6 Notice that $8 + 6 + 2 + 4 = 20$. Can you find four other numbers that equal 20?

8	1	6
3	5	7
4	9	2

ANOTHER MAGIC SQUARE

1 What is the sum of each row?

2 What is the sum of each column?

3 What is the sum of each diagonal?

4 What is the sum in the top left hand quarter of the square?

5 Can you find any more groups of four numbers that have the same sum?

1	14	4	15
8	11	5	10
13	2	16	3
12	7	9	6

MIRROR MATH

1   Use a mirror to complete these pictures:

2   Place a mirror on what you think is the axis of symmetry for each of these:

3   Use a mirror to read these words:

BIKE   BOB   BED

MAKE TEN

4	6	1	6
2	7	3	8
2	3	5	6
8	1	8	2

Use any three numbers that are near each other (either side by side or diagonally) to make 10, e.g. 4 + (2 × 3).

FIND THE SECRET NUMBER

1	2	3	4	5
6	7	8	9	10

Use each number once only; cross it out when it is used. Cross out:

a two numbers whose sum is 3

b two numbers whose product is 18

c two numbers whose sum is 18

d two numbers whose product is 45.

The secret number is the sum of the two remaining numbers. What is it?

SHAPE PUZZLE

Photocopy (or trace) these shapes and cut them out:

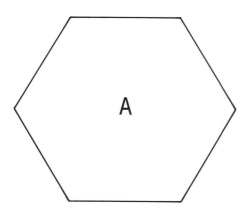
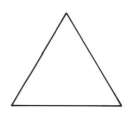
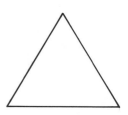

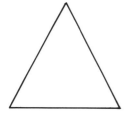
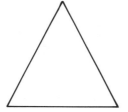
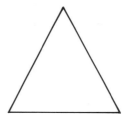
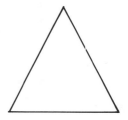

1 Use the hexagon (A) and the six triangles to make a six-pointed star.

2 Use the hexagon and some of the triangles to make:
  a a large triangle
  b a rhombus (diamond)
  c a shape with one axis of symmetry.

TESSELLATING PATTERNS

Fill each outline by drawing more of the same shape that is in it. (Do not overlap shapes and do not leave any gaps.)

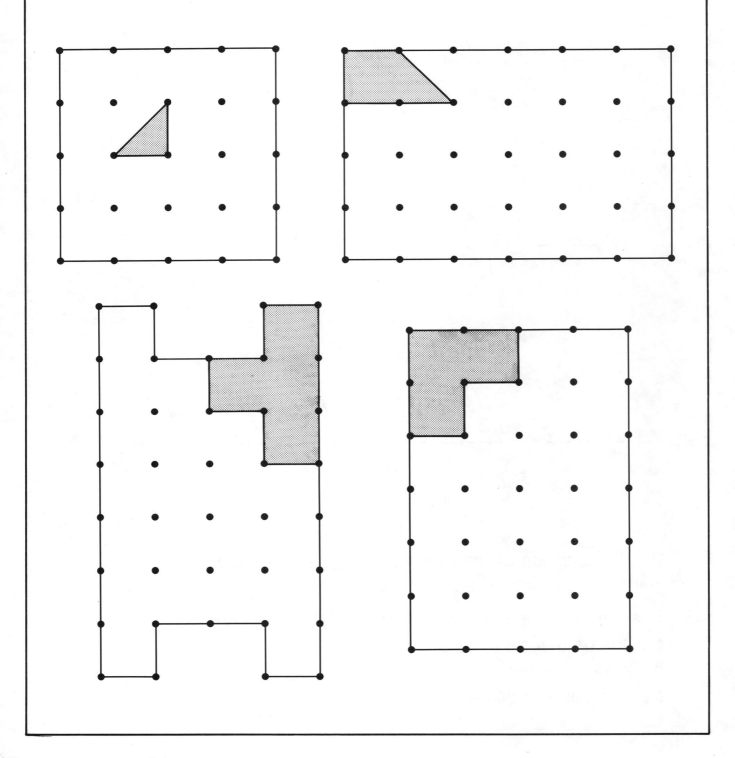

HOW MANY SQUARES?

1 Find five squares in this shape:

2 How many squares in this shape?

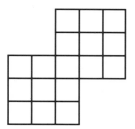

3 How many squares in this square mat?

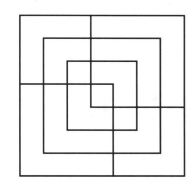

HOW MANY RECTANGLES?

1 Find six different rectangles in this:

2 How many rectangles in this shape?

3 How many rectangles in this shape?

MAKE THEM MATCH

Make a copy of these triangles:

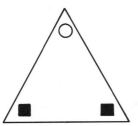 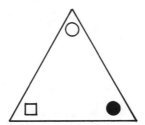 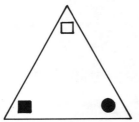 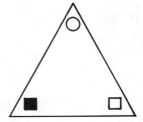

Can you fit them into this larger triangle so that the shapes in the corners of the small triangles match?

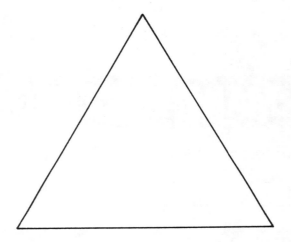

TRIANGLES

1   Obtain a box of toothpicks.

2   Can you form a triangle using three toothpicks?

3   Can you form a triangle using four toothpicks?

4   Can you make triangles from five toothpicks and from six toothpicks?

5   Can you make more than one kind of triangle with seven toothpicks?

JOINING DOTS

How many different-shaped triangles can you obtain by joining these dots in different ways?

FORMING SHAPES

1 Obtain a quantity of square tiles (all the same size). How many different kinds of shapes can you make using:

   a three squares

   b four squares?

2 Obtain some equilateral triangles (triangles with all their sides equal) of the same size. How many different shapes can you form using:

   a two of them

   b three of them

   c four of them?

3 Obtain some rectangles of the same shape and size. How many different shapes can you make using:

   a two of them

   b three of them?

PLACING BLOCKS

Play this game with a friend:

1 Obtain a set of attribute blocks. Pick out all the blue blocks and divide them up between you and your friend.

2 The player with the large thick blue square goes first and places it down on the floor.

3 Then the other player places beside it a block that differs in one way from it.

4 In turn, players continue to place in a line blue blocks differing in one way from the preceding one.

5 The winner is the first player to correctly place all of his or her blocks.

FIND THE SHAPE

1 Which two fit together to form a circle?

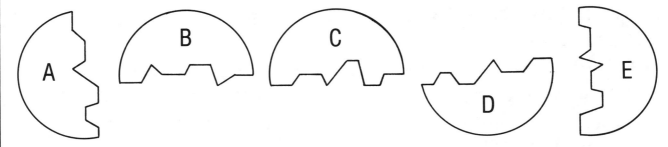

2 Which figure is the same as the first one?

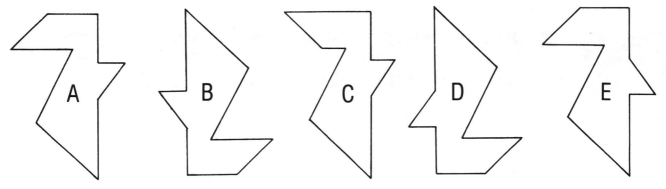

3 Match each of the descriptions (a to e) with its correct shape (i to v):

a All angles are right angles, not all sides are equal.

b All sides are equal, angles are equal, angles are not right angles.

c All sides are equal, all angles are right angles.

d All sides are equal, angles are not right angles, opposite angles are equal.

e None of the sides are equal, one pair of parallel sides.

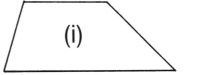

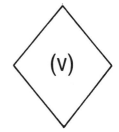

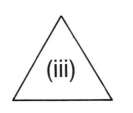

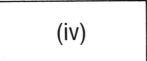

BACKWARDS AND FORWARDS

Palindromic numbers are numbers that read the same forwards and backwards, e.g. 33, 4224, 81518.

1 Make a list of all the palindromic numbers between 0 and 100.

2 Find all the palindromic numbers between 200 and 300.

3 How many times does a palindromic number occur on a digital watch between midnight and noon?

INTERESTING MULTIPLICATION

Complete these:

a   1 2 3 4 5 6 7 8 9
$$\times 8$$
_____
$$+ 9$$
_____

b   1 2 3 4 5 6 7 9
$$\times 3$$
_____
$$\times 9$$
_____

FUN WITH NINES

1 Complete the tables:

1	×	9	=	9		0	+	9	=	9
2	×	9	=	18		1	+	8	=	9
3	×	9	=	27		2	+	7	=	9
4	×	9	=	36		3	+	6	=	
5	×	9	=				+		=	
6	×	9	=				+		=	
7	×	9	=				+		=	
8	×	9	=				+		=	
9	×	9	=				+		=	
10	×	9	=				+		=	

2 How many different patterns can you find in the multiples of 9?

Fun with Nines — continued

3 You can use your fingers to help with the 9 times table:

Place your hands like this

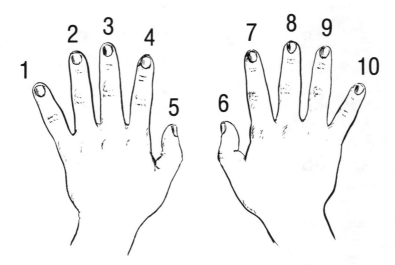

Now turn down the finger that matches the number of nines needed; e.g. if you want four 9s, turn down the fourth finger. The number of fingers to the left of the one turned down gives the tens digit, while the number to the right gives the units digit; e.g.

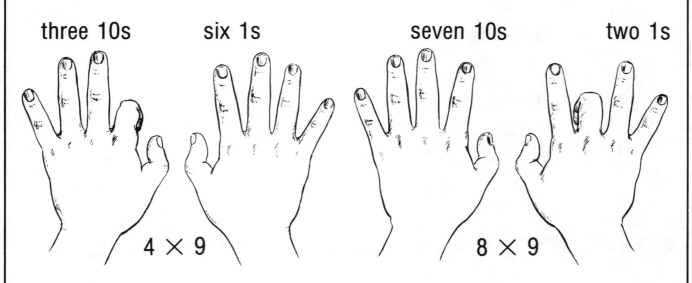

three 10s   six 1s   seven 10s   two 1s

4×9 8×9

Use your fingers to find 3×9, 7×9, 9×9, etc.

WHICH VIEW?

1 The following structure has a square base and the view from each side is:

Which of these is the top view?

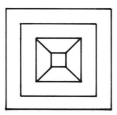 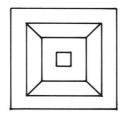 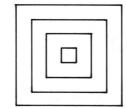 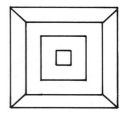

2 The following structure also has a square base; the view from each side is:

Draw the top view.

3 This is the top view of a structure with a square base:

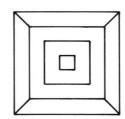

Draw a side view of it.

WHICH ONES?

1 These are GEOPS

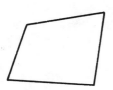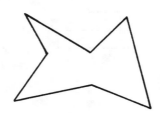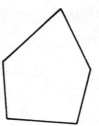

These are not GEOPS

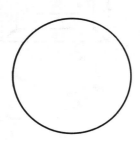

Which are GEOPS?

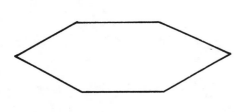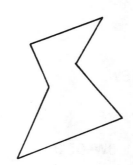

2 What is a DIGON?

   a is one

   b is not

   c is one

   d is one

   e is not

Which out of f, g, h are DIGONS?

a  **b** **c**

d **e** **f**

g **h**

FINDING PATTERNS

Look at the numbers:

1   3   7   13   21

To help us find a pattern, complete these:

$1 + \underline{} = 3,$ $3 + \underline{} = 7,$
$7 + \underline{} = 13,$ $13 + \underline{} = 21$

What must be added to 21 to find the next number?

Find the next number in each of these:

a   3,   5,   7,   9,   ___
b   1,   5,   9,   13,   ___
c   1,   2,   4,   7,   11,   ___
d   1,   2,   4,   8,   16,   ___
e   1,   4,   9,   16,   ___
f   2,   5,   11,   23,   ___
g   2,   5,   10,   17,   ___
h   1,   11,   20,   28,   ___
i   1,   2,   6,   15,   31,   ___
j   2,   4,   9,   17,   28,   ___

FIGURE PATTERNS

1 Study these figures and notice how the shaded part moves from one part to the next in a clockwise direction:

2 Now complete these in the same way:

a   **?**

b   **?**

c   **?**

d   **?**

e   **?**

f   **?**

g   **?**

h   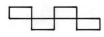 **?**

PUZZLES WITH CUBES

1 How many small cubes are needed to build these solids?

 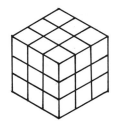  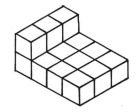

2 Trace (or photocopy) this net and use it to make a cube:

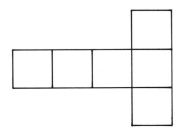

3 Which of these will form cubes?

a 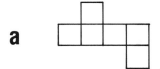   **b** 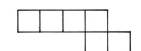   **c**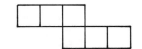

4 This net was used to make a cube.
The cube is placed in different positions as shown below:

In each case what is on the blank face?

PLACING SHAPES

1 Trace (or photocopy) these shapes and cut them out:

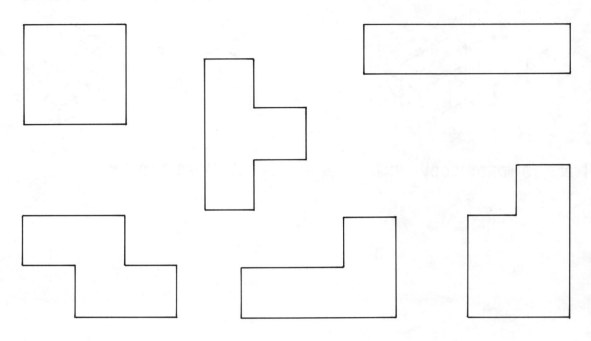

2 Use three of the shapes to cover this shape:

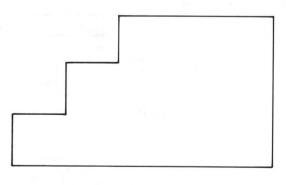

3 Use the six shapes to cover this square:

WORK BACKWARDS

1 What number did I start with in the following:

□ times 8 minus 18 divided by 6 plus 3 is 8.

2 Today I have 12 canaries in my aviary. Yesterday 4 escaped when the door was left open. Three days ago I sold half of what I had. How many did I sell?

3 Joe traveled up 8 floors. He then walked down stairs for 3 floors, got in the elevator and went up 5 floors, then walked down stairs for 4 floors. If he finished at the 12th floor, at what floor did he start?

MISSING NUMBERS

Find the missing numbers:

	7	9	8	5
+ 3			11	
−	2			
×			32	

Possible answers

(in some cases there are others)

Hit the target (p.3)
2. 10, 10, 0 or 10, 5, 5

Three threes (p.7)
$3 + 3 + 3 = 9$
$3 + 3 - 3 = 3$
$(3+3) \div 3 = 2$
$3 \times 3 - 3 = 6$
$3 \times 3 + 3 = 12$
$(3+3) \times 3 = 18$
$(3-3) \times 3 = 0$
$3 \times 3 \times 3 = 27$
$(3 \div 3) + 3 = 4$

Patterns and sequences (p.8)
2 1,2,4,8,16,32 (*doubling*)
4 1,3,6,10,15,21 (*add 1 more each time*)

Number puzzles 1 (p.10)
1 HELP FIRE CALL 911
2 35 63 120 77

Number puzzles 2 (p.11)
2 5 *or* 6 *or* 4
614   534   256
 2   2   3
 3   1   1

6 1,4,5,8 *in inner square*
2,3,6,7 *in outer square*

Number puzzles 3 (p.12)
2 18 ($=5+1+6+1+5$)

Cutting a pizza (p.13)
a 16 pieces

Math path addition (p.16)

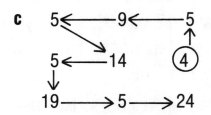

What am I? (p.21)
2 24 (with factors of 2,3,4,6,8,12)

Break the code (p.21)
1 729

Dot paper shapes (p.22)
e

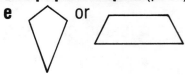

Further number puzzles (1) (p.23)
3 $5 + 4 - 3 = 6$
$1 + 3 - 2 = 2$
$4 \times 2 - 8 = 0$

Further number puzzles (2) (p.24)
2 4 1 3   **4** 6 3 8
6 2 5   2 1 5
                 9 4 7

Further number puzzles (3) (p.25)
7 J=8, L=4, P=1, Q=2, O=0
8 3 $5 notes and 1 $10 note

Find the pattern (p.26)
c 15 (double, minus 1)
e 15 (square, minus 1)

Numbers for letters (p.26)

b 12 *or* 2 1
    45   3 6

c 4 3 1
    1 5 2
    5 8 3

Hidden numbers (p.28)

3 1 5
6 4 8
9 2 7

Where are they? (p.31)

Lunch orders (p.33)

       Sue
Salad	$1.95
Cake	.75
Drink	.72
	$3.42

Find the secret number (p.36)

11 (4 + 7)

How many squares (p.39)

2 27
3 16

Make them match (p.40)

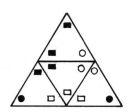

Find the shape (p.43)

1 A *and* D

Backwards and forwards (p.44)

3 57 times
      (12.21,1.01,1.11,1.21,...1.51,
      2.02,......9.59,10.01,11.11)

Notes for teachers

Hit the target (p.3)
In each of questions 2 and 3 there is more than one possible answer. [Not all shots need score.]

Three in a line (p.6)
Some suppliers of school materials stock wooden cubes, from which you can easily make dice (by writing on their six faces).

Number puzzles (1) (p.10)
1 Pupils should replace the numbers in each cell of the grid with a letter, e.g. 7×8 by H ($=56$).
2 A clue is to look for number reversals, e.g. 43 and 34.
3 A clue is to look at the number of dots in each cell.
4 Start with the units.

Number puzzles (2) (p.11)
1 A clue is to place '3' in the central circle.

Cutting a pizza (p.13)
This is an excellent example for demonstrating problem-solving strategies:
a consider simpler cases;
b draw diagrams;
c compile tables;
d search for a pattern.

Exploring with tangrams (p.14)
Pupils can find that shapes C, D, and E can each be covered by the two small triangles (A and B); this implies that C, D, and E each have the same area.

Tangram puzzles (p.15)
You may make many more like these by simply forming any shape (with your seven tangram pieces) and tracing around it.

Math path addition (p.16)
Simply circle the starting number and use arrows to indicate the path followed.
(You can make some for subtraction and/or for multiplication.)

Target prime (p.17)
This game provides experience in forming number sentences (combining numbers to obtain a target number). It also emphasizes those numbers that are prime, e.g. 2, 3, 5, 7, 11, . . .

Sand trap (p.18)
This provides simple introductory experience with coordinates.

Race to one (p.18)
This is an excellent game for providing practice in finding factors of numbers. It is a quick-moving game and can be played often.

Poly-color (p.19)
This game encourages problem-

solving as pupils search for the best strategy to employ.

Find the winner (p.20)
Pupils should draw a line and place marks along it to represent 10-meter intervals. Place Sue somewhere in the middle. Then place Pam, Rick, Bob, and Jill.

How many steps? (p.20)
A diagram helps.

What can she buy? (p.20)
Encourage pupils to estimate cost of purchases, e.g. for (a) 3 meters of material at $6 per meter.

Break the code (p.21)
These examples provide experience in numeration using unfamiliar symbols.

Find the pattern (p.26)
Ask pupils to find what has been done to each number in the left column to obtain the corresponding number in the right column, e.g. 3 has been added to each or each has been multiplied by 4 or each has been doubled and then 1 has been subtracted.

Numbers for letters (p.26)
The same number must be used for the same letter in a given example (but not necessarily from one example to the next).

Hidden numbers (p.28)
As a starting clue use the fact that the sum of column 2 is 7; this

implies that column 2 must contain 1, 2 and 4.

Lunch orders (p.33)
These may be solved partly by noting likely combinations and partly by trial and error.

Tessellating patterns (p.38)
Look for tessellations in the environment, e.g. tiles on floors. [Congruent shapes (shapes of the same size and shape) tessellate when they fit together without leaving gaps or without overlapping.]

Forming shapes (p.41)
1 If you insist that the tiles share an entire edge in common with each other, then you should find that there are
   a two different shapes formed when using three tiles,
   b five different shapes formed when using four tiles.

Placing blocks (p.42)
As a variation you could play a 2-difference game (with each block differing in exactly two ways from the preceding one).

Puzzles with cubes (p.51)
1 Pupils could model these using small wooden cubes (if available).
   b Tabs (for gluing) could be attached to every second edge.
   c Pupils could use interlocking squares (such as Polydron squares).